They Said I Could Be Anything I Wanted

a collection of thoughts and poetry

Sofía Ramírez Castillo

India | USA | UK

Made with ❤ on the BookLeaf Publishing Platform
www.bookleafpub.in
www.bookleafpub.com

Dedication

Uncle Henry,

The world feels lost and broken without you. You were a beacon of light, adventure, and inspiration to us, and we will continue to make you proud.

Please remember to visit us every now and then. I'll be waiting in my dreams with a glass of wine to gossip about our family and discuss the beauty and importance of being a Hufflepuff.

We miss you now and will miss you forever. We hope you're still riding your bike in the clouds—I'm sure the view is spectacular.

I love you.

-La Petite Sophie

Preface

The following pages offer a direct line of access to the author's thoughts, ideas, self-reflections, and deepest fears. The writer in question loves playing with words and evoking feelings on a page, but still, she must confess that she has never formally studied poetry, writing, or literature, apart from the introductory courses she took in school. This means that this work is not only a labor of love but also of complete honesty and vulnerability. If you are a literary enthusiast familiar with the rules of poetry, and the structural components of the poems are imperfect, she sincerely apologizes, as the rules of poetry are foreign to her. But what she wrote is genuine, and she promises that these printed words serve as a one-way ticket to her heart and often wandering mind, so please tread carefully.

I must confess that the poet in question is me. I assume you've figured that out already, but it feels important to say it outright. After all, this book is all about trust. I trust you, the readers, to take care of the most precious things I possess: my thoughts, opinions, and treasured stories. Please take the time to read these simple verses because while I may have written them with a specific intention, my hope is that you might find an interpretation of your own. Ultimately, this comes down to my voice and what I need to express, but most importantly, the feelings and debates they evoke in you. I hope you enjoy this book. For you, this book may represent complete chaos, but for me, it's a way to immortalize my feelings in the most vulnerable manner.

Acknowledgements

While for many years, I held a "me against the world" attitude, life has shown me several times that this philosophy doesn't work. Over time, I've come to realize that I need people, and surprisingly, other people need me too. I attributed this mindset and all my other flawed qualities to suffering from an extraneous case of only-child syndrome- it's a real thing. But alas, that excuse only takes you so far, and life once again emphasized that human beings can change and that I am not, nor have I ever been, alone. Long story short, I've matured a bit and discovered that it's much more enjoyable to let go of anger toward the world and try to have a little bit of fun. Most things are not that serious.
Now that you have read my self-assessed psychological profile, we can move on to the actual acknowledging portion of this book.

To my parents, thank you for never leaving my side. Your unconditional support, even when I was pursuing genuinely insane, irresponsible, and ridiculous ideas, has always made me feel loved and invincible. I've always felt safe and protected with you by my side, and you taught me how to protect and defend myself, too, for which I am eternally grateful. I would be nothing without you.

To my grandma, Anabelle, you are the strongest person I know. You are kind-hearted and an incredible role model. Seeing how I've grown up to be like you fills me with pride.
To my grandfather, Carlos, thank you for your sense of adventure and eternal curiosity for the world. I would travel anywhere with you.

While it feels a little corny, and I'm not one to be too sentimental, I also want to acknowledge myself. Despite my unrealistic expectations and the many times I have been unkind to my mind and body, I always pick myself up and try again, and that is all I can ask for. All the failures and disappointments have done nothing but teach me lessons, and at the risk of sounding arrogant or immodest, which is genuinely not my intention, I am in awe of what I have accomplished so far. Sometimes, it's important for me to recognize my achievements and remember to give myself a break. After all, I am trying my best. Now, enough about me. Let's move on.

Finally, to my other half: Goose (and just to clarify for those who have never met us, your real name is Jose, but it will be a cold day in hell before I call you that). You have shown me a love and kindness that feels foreign to me. You are my perfect gentleman, and I am honored to be your partner. You challenge me to be better every day because you believe I can do and be anything I want. For that, I will be forever thankful. I am proud to be yours, and I am proud of you. Thank you for choosing me to be your happy ending.

And last but not least, to my readers, if we have never met, it's a pleasure to finally meet you. Thank you for taking the time to read my thoughts. I hope I didn't bore you too much, as I often struggle to follow a coherent thread in my own mind. I sincerely hope you enjoy my poems and that you come back. As you may know, life only gets harder as we age, which can be scary and uncomfortable, but finding spaces that can serve as an escape to help us unwind and regroup from ourselves and others is essential. I hope my writing can be a safe space for you. You are the reason authors get to do what they love. You are the heart of the literary industry. Without you, we are nothing. Thank you for bringing us such joy.

1. Traveling Thoughts

I want the things I have to say to matter
For my thoughts and ideas to travel the world and for
people to care about them
And not because I deem myself important; I don't care
for recognition
But because I wish to say that I get it

That fame and followers don't matter
That media is nothing more than a cruel facade that asks
for unattainable perfection
A fake, nonexistent image
That feasts on a cesspool of insecurities and comparisons

And that, in the end, it's all a meaningless notion
Because we are all uncertain fools dancing in a
masquerade for deception

2. Labels are a Man Made Construct

I've spent countless mornings and infinite afternoons
drowning in my own queries
Who am I?
Does publishing this book make me a poet?
Does killing an ant make me a murderer?
Who has the right to decide who I am if I don't even
have that privilege myself?

I have many dreams to live before I go
I want to dance with a Spanish poet
Skinny dip on the vast Arctic Ocean
And drink bitter coffee under the crescent moonlight
I want to be everything and nothing all at once

What makes me anything?
When I was a kid, people asked me what I wanted to be
when I grew up
They said I could be anything I wanted
All I ever wanted was to be happy

3. A Galaxy of Forgotten Ideas

Last night in bed, I thought of a poem
And in the matter and transaction of falling asleep
I lost it
And it made me wonder
How many great ideas are lost to a galaxy of dreams we
barely remember?

4. I Wish I'd Been Friends with Neruda

Last year, while backpacking through South America
I ended up in the capital of Chile
Walking down cobblestone streets
I turned left on Fernando Márquez De La Plata
And found the home that gave farewell to a literary
legend

That afternoon, after aimless wondering
I walked into Neruda's house
Where he spent his last decades with the woman he
loved
I toured La Chascona with curious eyes
And read the legacies of his own handwriting

I felt inspired-
Walking through his study and resting my hand on the
surface of his desk
I imagined myself a Chilean poet
With a whiskey in one hand and a pen in the other
I'd buy myself an old beret

I'd be quick with my words and say romantic, off-the-
top-of-my-head phrases

Savoring expensive smoke from an old Cuban cigar
And I'd hope people would listen to the words coming
from my heart
Oftentimes, I wonder if I'd be interesting enough
Would I ever be good enough to be worthy of Neruda's
attention?

I imagine myself under his tutelage, swapping stories in
an old cafe
If I had been born in the 1900s
If I had Neruda's bravery and determination
His raw talent and vulnerability to play with Spanish
words
I think I could've been a great Chilean poet

5. The Scientific Method of an Inevitable Ending

After failed hypotheses and successful observations
I've deduced there is only a singular, universal fear that
holds ground
And it's not heights, darkness, crickets or cancer
It's the fear of Death itself

It's the fear of exhausting all occidental medicine
without curing a single symptom
The fear of slipping into a 30-foot drop that ends in a
layer of concrete cement
The fear that in the absence of light, the unknown can
hurt us

These are all just mere manifestations of the originating
cause
Of the crippling, logical, ever-expanding terror of dying
and therefore ceasing to be

6. Grief is a Constant Reminder

I've just recently had an intimate experience with grief
that has left me suspended
Paralyzed in a constant state of nothingness
But I've learned to accept the feeling as a part of
everyday life
And embrace the numbness that comes with it

I understand that it's a process
Slow and poignant
A constant reminder that something is missing
That time continues, and life theoretically goes on, but a
part of you won't
And it's the method of learning how life will be from
that moment on

It's genuinely painful and rather uncomfortable
But at the same time, it can be a blessing
A constant reminder that someone was there
That those who leave us take a little piece of our hearts
with them
And that even though we are incomplete, those are the
pieces that will eventually lead us back to heaven
To finally reunite with the people we've missed

7. I'm Too Bored to Even Name This Simple Poem

Today, I find myself bored
I am indifferent, and mean, and reluctant to comply
I am careless with other people,
I don't seem to mind hurting their feelings, valid as they may be
I don't like this version of myself

Today, I feel rude and apathetic
Others put up with it in the name of patience
I know it's a lot to ask,
And they don't owe me anything
But not every day can be a good one

Boredom is a funny thing
It's rooted in a feeling of discomfort within yourself
Distractions are a temporary cure
Motivation is its nemesis
But where do I find the motivation to fight it when I am bored out of my mind?

8. The Agonizing Chase of an Insufficient Satisfaction

Not once in my life have I taken up a hobby,
That provides me with instant satisfaction
I always find myself doing activities that frustrate me
Activities that challenge me both physically and
mentally
And leave me wondering if I'll ever be decent enough

Sometimes, I fear that I started too late and I'm running
out of time
I see other girls my age doing spectacular things while
I'm still taking my first steps
But then I ask myself if I'd like to quit to appease these
crippling doubts
And the answer is no

I want to struggle
I want to feel the frustration diffidence
And prove to myself that I've always been capable

I feel inadequate sometimes
And I hate myself for having that mentality
I want to believe in me like others do and feel as
invincible as I know I can be

And that's why I keep going
That's why I keep following passions that push me to my
limit
Because quitting was never an option, and the mountain
of success is never-ending
And once I climb to the top, I need to see what's next
That is, precisely, what keeps me alive in an endless
conquest to see how far I'll go

9. Winter Dread from a Japanese Perspective

Dried maple leaves fall
Anxious shivers through my heart
Learned to hate winter

10. Welcome to The Greatest Show on Earth

Under a worn-out, old red and white striped tent, I found
my home
The raggedy string lights zigzagging above the audience
were my stage
The deafening applause, my drug of choice
And the smell of stale popcorn and roasted peanuts gave
me a permanent sense of belonging

The clowns and jugglers were my friends
But the trapeze was my partner
My heart beat to the rhythm of carnival music and
buzzing laughter

The traveling life is not for everyone
But it's the only lifestyle I ever knew
The circus always brings damaged souls together
And within its madness, we formed our broken family

11. Wildfire of Resentment

Old wise men say to forgive but to never forget
They'd rather hold an everlasting grudge,
Forever keep a poisoned memory
As a constant and hurtful reminder that they were
wronged

But in my spirit of causeless rebelliousness,
I choose to disagree
I choose to let go of all anger and resentment
To free myself of a self-subjected suffering that slowly
kills me

Resentment spreads like wildfire through a dead,
forgotten forest
The all-consuming flames transform into hate
Leaving an empty shell of a man who forgot the power
of forgiveness
I choose to say no

I want to forgive, and I need to forget
I'd rather live content and free than be dragged down by
my bitter antipathy
Because mistakes are lessons in disguise

And I'd rather move on and shed foreign guilt than

sentence myself to a loathsome existence

14

12. We're Bound to "Thrive" in a Self-Centered, Ungrateful, Earth-Murdering Society

Do you think candles feel the scorching heat when they melt?
Do the cabinets scream when we slam their wooden doors?
I think of humanity and all the little actions we take that harbor a massive reaction
And I ask myself, who entrusted us with so much power?

Who thought it was okay to torch millions of trees and execute thousands of forests,
Leaving animals homeless and humans unoxygenated to build the next apartment complex?
Who decided recycling was a scam,
And that the ocean was running low on plastic?

When did we become so obsessed with ourselves
That we thought we could disrupt the natural order of the universe?

I want to know the exact date and time
That we decided as a society to murder the planet that
raised us

13. It Wasn't London After All

London that night was restless
The lampposts flickered on her shoulders
A drunken haze hummed in the night
Carnaby Street was full of life
But she felt dead inside

She walked into a club hoping for companionship
But the place was too crowded
The bodies too sweaty
The noise too deafening
Her breath quickened

She shut her eyes to slow her heartbeat
Beads of sweat coating her palms
The inside of her cheek began to bleed as she bit away
scar tissue in a fruitless attempt to calm herself
Her quivering hands pressed against her ears, forming
an aching pressure on her temples
She willed the noise to stop-

And suddenly, it did
She let out a slow breath
Felt her lungs compressing

And when she finally forced her eyes open
She realized the room was always empty

14. Who Wants to Live Forever?

Often times when the night is quiet, and I can hear my thoughts
I absentmindedly begin to imagine selfish things
I think of our story and how desperately I love you
And realize I don't want to live without you
I quietly hope it's a reciprocated feeling

How poetic and to some romantic would it be
Since we started our adventure at such a young age
If we wrote our next chapter together
If our hearts gave out at the same time and we took our last breath in synchrony
To walk eternity together, like we always did, hand in hand

I secretly wonder if you'd like that

15. Death Is an Old Friend

I've always liked to wander around cemeteries
In a world drowning in anxiety and despair
I like the peace and quiet of the past
The dead offer a company that's often filled with solace

I'm surrounded by a thousand lifetimes
On the one hand, ancient ghosts drag themselves around
me, reciting old sorrows like a broken mantra
All the what-ifs and could-have-been are buried in the
ground
Covered by withered flowers and forgotten memories

On the other, children stuck in a perpetual youth run
circles around me
Unbothered by unfulfilled dreams of an old age
Instead, they laugh and play and build castles in the dirt
And every morning, they watch the sunrise as they
welcome a new day in their eternal childhood

16. Age Has a Bitter Taste

I would love to be able to see the world as a child
To have a curiosity for everything and not fear anything
at all
From when I thought I was invincible and could conquer
the world
Back when life was simple

Now I'm old and mistrusting of others
I think twice before making any decision
Everything feels like it's too much around me
And I feel small, fragile, like a broken glass

Back then, I used to run everywhere
With the eternal notion of finding the yellow butterflies,
García Márquez wrote about
Now I am exhausted and resentful of younger
generations
Because I know I've lost my chances, and they've just
started theirs

17. A Light Was Born

On the early morning of March 17th, a light was born
He was magic
Fifty-six years later, on November 25th, that light burnt out,
Taking ours with it

Looking up at the night, I wonder where you are
I imagine angels laughing with you, and I'm jealous
But it comforts me to know that your magic still prevails
Because only a smile as incandescent can eclipse a full moon in a magnitude of colors
A disoriented rooster announces a new day as birds sing your favorite tunes, and I relish in your memory
And it hurts

Your absence feels everlasting, and I'm stuck in a loophole of melancholy and fear,
Surrounded by broken loved ones
Time was- *is* cruel and unkind
We miss you

I spent days fighting against grief and making it my enemy,
Trying to protect my heart from shattering,

By accepting the inevitable truth that you're gone, but I
lost the fight
No one wins the war against Death
She's invincible

So now, I have decided to celebrate grief,
To accept its discomfort and embrace its lessons
I'll surrender myself to it entirely,
Understanding with crystal clear clarity that it has to
break me for it to release me

Every time the thought of losing you catches my breath,
I will hold still for a moment and think of you
Your bike rides by the ocean and irrefutable spirit of love
and adventure
An ode to your life and everything you stood for
And I will feel okay

Adopting grief as a part of my penance
While transforming it into a treasured reminder that I
got to know you
That we got to coincide on this Earth, and I had the
honor of sharing your blood
God, I'm so lucky

Suddenly, the stinging feeling of pain is welcome,
And accompanied by a profound and infinite sense of

pride
Infinitely proud of being your niece and infinitely proud
of your legacy
I am infinitely proud of you

On the early morning of March 17th, a light was born
Fifty-six years later, on November 25th, that light
became an eclipse,
Strong enough to accompany us as we navigate this all-
encompassing grief
We love you

18. It's a Poet Thing

Are poets meant to be perpetually nostalgic?
I think about this often
This afternoon, I sat down facing the lake
With the full intention of writing an uplifting poem
And I failed miserably

I started well
I thought of a girl that met a boy
And when they passed one another at the train station
They promised to meet that afternoon at four o'clock for
what could be the start of their love story
She was ready by three fifteen, excited and hopeful for a
new beginning

But suddenly she heard a thunder, and it all came back
The rain, the crash, the fear, the pain
And a soul-crushing anxiety left her paralyzed at her
doorstep
She felt her stomach sink as she wished for the boy at
the coffee shop not to hate her
And she wondered if she'd ever know love or if her fate
was destined to be cursed for the rest of her life

19. Creativity Was Never a Good Fit for Grown-Up, Professional Matters

How many creative people
Entrepreneurs in comedy and the arts
Are wasted in office jobs and can barely afford rent,
Sad and frustrated because they've never been given a chance?

I once read of a comedian who worked as a public accountant
One day, the office decided it wanted to maximize its revenue
And determined that the comedian's salary was expendable
The comedian, freed from office responsibilities and counting other people's money
Walked up to a stage and chose to face his fearful doubts

The other advisors, consultants, and analysts dragged their feet aimlessly
Thinking of a parallel universe in which they followed their dreams
And in a fruitless search to find a magic cure for their

useless depression
They walked into a bar, and instead of a beer, they found
a comedian in need of an audience

And just like that, frustration and anguish met a hopeful
dreamer
And in between jokes and stories
The audience found their laughter, and the comedian
found his passion

And just like the comedian, there have been many others
Authors and musicians who left the comfort of a
mediocre salary
For the opportunity to chase their dreams

Those are, precisely, the people I admire
Not the ones with millions in their bank accounts
But the ones with millions of stories about how they
became happy

Long live comedians and entrepreneurs of joy!
Some days will be great, and others will be miserable
But regardless of the risk of an uncertain future
They have the peace and certainty of knowing that they
are truly living-
Living an honest life in the pursuit of an epic adventure

And that is all that ever mattered

28

20. Poetry Is Everywhere

Yesterday, I read that poetry could be found in moments
That the smell of fresh coffee can be an art
The sun's warmth on my skin could be a treasure
And that laughter was music

So this morning, I woke up intending to search for these
moments
And I was surprised to find that the act of waking up
itself left me breathless
I thought about every star that had to align for me to be
here
I thought about all of the atoms and molecules that
worked together to create me
And I was speechless

At six in the morning, I opened my eyes and concluded
While poetry is found in small moments
Poetry is also found in me

21. An Innocent Response from a Female Perspective on the First of the Twenty Love Poems a Chilean Legend Once Wrote

His hands are rough and calloused
He has an advantage in strength and height
I don't want to be here
I want to run out and feel the breeze caressing my chest
Even though I'm barefoot and my feet are bleeding with
every step, I want to be free
I want to belong to myself again

I find myself living in a perpetual hell
In which I was handed off to the world, and it wasn't my
own decision
My cries and desperate pleas were silenced by the weight
of a threat
And a piercing pressure in my womb

I spend my time obsessively thinking about memories of
when we were happy

When consent was a silent word because,
Between intimate laughs and covert glances
We created our own secret language

But nothing is the same anymore
The love we had escaped us
We searched for it tirelessly
But after all that aimless searching, our hearts grew tired
We came back to an empty house,
Locked within four barren walls that held our hopeless
aspirations

I am miserable and exhausted
I sleep next to a stranger
Someone that I used to know but I haven't recognized in
a long time
And I cry in silence

I no longer have any say in the matter
And it seems to me that I will be destined to kiss these
forceful lips
Until the day finally comes when love taps my window
And gives me the strength to say -
Enough